HEADLINES III:
NOT THE MOVIE, STILL THE BOOK

REAL BUT RIDICULOUS SAMPLINGS FROM AMERICA'S NEWSPAPERS

COMPILED BY JAY LENO

WITH PHOTOGRAPHS BY JOSEPH DEL VALLE AND CARTOONS BY JACK DAVIS

WARNER BOOKS

A Time Warner Company

All author royalties will be donated to the Samuel Jared Kushnick Foundation, which funds pediatric A.I.D.S. programs and pediatric immunology research.

Warner Books, Inc., 666 Fifth Avenue, New York, NY 10103

 A Time Warner Company

Printed in the United States of America
First printing: December 1991
10 9 8 7 6 5 4 3 2 1

Library of Congress Cataloging-in-Publication Data

Headlines III : not the movie, still the book : real but ridiculous
samplings from America's newspapers / compiled by Jay Leno ; with
photographs by Joseph Del Valle and cartoons by Jack Davis.
   p.   cm.
   ISBN 0–446–39374–6
   1. Newspapers—Headlines—Humor. 2. American wit and humor.
I. Leno, Jay. II. Title: Headlines 3. III. Title: Headlines three.
PN6231.N6H43   1991
081—dc20   91–14829
                                             CIP

Cover design by Jackie Merri Meyer/Robert Cuevas
Cover photograph by Joseph Del Valle
Book design by Giorgetta Bell McRee

With the publication of the third book of HEADLINES, we would like to take this opportunity to thank you for your support of pediatric A.I.D.S. programs not only through your purchase of these books but by taking the time to send these headlines to Jay.

Please know that over the past three years, 100 percent of all the author's royalties from these books have gone directly to many organizations. Childrens' hospitals and related support programs throughout the country have been the beneficiary of your generosity.

You have made a difference.

Sincerely,

SAMUEL JARED KUSHNICK FOUNDATION

BRILLIANT DEDUCTIONS

With investigative techniques that rival Sherlock Holmes's, today's scientists are peeling back the layers of knowledge—arriving at undreamed-of discoveries. Take the following headlines, for example...

Smaller families require less food

So that would mean bigger families require more food? I'm confused.

Farmers buy most farmland

WASHINGTON — Through thick and thin, the biggest buyers of farmland are other farmers, says an Agriculture Department report.

Gee, I wonder what they do with it?

Ability to swim may save children from drowning

I guess we'll just have to use bigger weights.

Sewers are not good playgrounds

Sounds like just another overprotective mom.

Americans are unlikely to give up eating during recession

Jail crowding caused by increase in criminals, new study concludes

Let's not jump to any conclusions.

Panel hears specialist testify — women's breasts not like men's

I'd like more time to study this case.

DID I READ THAT RIGHT?

The job of the family newspaper is not to misdirect readers—as supermarket tabloids sometimes do—but inform. Occasionally, though, they just can't help it...

Attorneys don't want ban on lawyer-client sex

SACRAMENTO (AP) — California attorneys were ordered to draft rules limiting their sexual behavior after claims that a famed divorce attorney raped two clients, but critics say the proposed regulations are too liberal.

Now there's a shock.

"Girls will be girls" department:

Nuclear winter may not be so bad

Yeah, and playing in the sewer is a lot of fun, too.

Blind Cabbie Forced To Abandon Driving

Now he can go back to his day job as an umpire.

"Luckily the bomb sustained little damage" department:

Bomb hit
by library

Mimes banned for abusive language

CLEVELAND HEIGHTS—
The San Francisco Mime troupe was banned from performing at Heights High School after school officials said they didn't like the language used in the production.

It's not *what* they said, it's *how* they said it.

Ten Commandments declared obsolete by 'news king' Turner

TV mogul issues his own 10 rules

I guess if you've broken them all, they *are* obsolete.

State will poison rivers so it can count dead fish

Hey, this doesn't have anything to do with that "all-you-can-eat" fish fry, does it?

Some men retain mental ability

Here's one feminists may dispute.

**"Hey, wait a minute. I don't remember reading that in the catalogue"
department:**

Univ. Of Michigan Mulls Neutering Its Freshmen

Train towed after collision with '83 Buick

PEEKSKILL — When a turbo-charged Amtrak engine slammed into  in his '83 Buick on Tuesday morning, ████████ was able to walk away.

The Buick suffered some damage to a front fender, but the locomotive was dead in its tracks.

It's a good thing it wasn't a '59 Cadillac. Everybody on that train would have been killed!

Sperm tax

OTTAWA — The federal goods and services tax (GST) is angering an unlikely segment of the population — women undergoing donor insemination. Women and couples will now be charged the GST on donated sperm.

Good luck trying to collect.

Post office paychecks get lost in mail

What goes around comes around.

"Maybe you should grow a beard" department:

'Hole in face' sends man to hospital

~~XXXXXXXXX~~, 21, of College Station was shot in the left side of his face while walking in the Highland Courts housing project about 10:30 p.m. Wednesday, but didn't realize he had "a hole in his face" until the following day, he told Little Rock police.

Animal-rights group to hold meeting at steakhouse

GREAT FALLS, Mont. (AP) — An animal-rights group that hopes to change Americans' meat-eating ways scheduled a meeting here today at the Black Angus steakhouse.

Before I begin the meeting, let me have two lamb chops, one New York sirloin, and a pork loin.

"Just say neigh" department:

Man pleads innocent to charges of sexual assault on horse

An Itawamba County man accused in a string of sexual assaults on Lee County horses pleaded innocent to four related charges at his arraignment Monday in Lee County Circuit Court.

████████████████████████ ██████████, pleaded innocent to having intercourse with an animal, killing a quarter horse, grand larceny in connection with the abduction of a Shetland pony and destruction of private property in connection with another assault.

Solid Waste, Recycling to be Dinner Topic

Hey, why don't we meet at that steakhouse?

Woman unsure how she sat on pork chop bone

NASHVILLE — Julia ~~Schmansky~~ is more careful about where she sits after doctors looking for cancer found a pork chop bone in her derriere.

Doctors removed the 4-'inch bone last October from the left cheek on her buttocks and estimate the bone had been there between five and 10 years.

"They thought it was a tumor, and instead of finding a tumor they found a pork chop bone," Mrs. ~~Schmansky, 64, of Nashville,~~ said recently.

The *good* news, ma'am, is that you don't have hemorrhoids...

Angry, jobless Santas picket mall after elf accused of lechery

West Seneca, N.Y.

Santa Claus walked a picket line Friday after a company that provides Santas was fired by mall managers because an elf allegedly made a suggestive comment to a store employee.

Jingle bells, jingle bells, jingle all...

Teen births in Brevard up 17 percent, study says

Birth rate dropping among Brevard teens

This is what happens when you send two reporters to cover the same story.

Passenger trains hurt by lack of track

WASHINGTON — Passenger rail service across much of the country is being threatened by a lack of suitable track.

Uh-oh, what's that com—
Hey! Look out for that '83 Buick!!!

Customers didn't notice dead clerk

Excuse me, can you help me?...
Uh, excuse me...excuse me...

Gas chamber executions may be health hazard

You know, I think it's true.
Everyone who's used it is dead now.

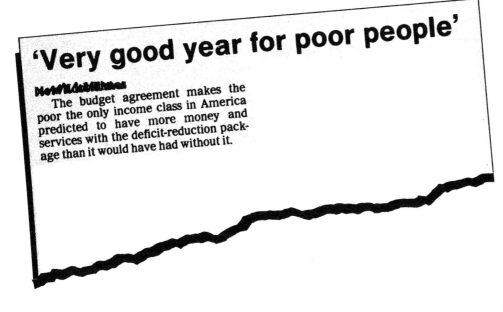

'Very good year for poor people'

~~How I Made Millions~~

The budget agreement makes the poor the only income class in America predicted to have more money and services with the deficit-reduction package than it would have had without it.

It's been a *great* year for them.
Look how many more of them there are.

Missing turtle turns up after 13 years

LONDON (AP) — An Oriental soft shell turtle, presumed dead for 13 years, has been found alive and well in her compartment at a zoo in Devon, the curator says.

~~xxxxxxxxx~~ said the turtle, who disappeared in 1976 from Paignton Zoo, 130 miles southwest of London, was found hiding in a silted pond after a gardener spotted her stealing meat. The turtle is now full size with a large, bobbing neck and a 12-inch grey, soft, pliant shell.

Zookeepers were amazed at its excellent condition especially since the turtle's primary diet is meat and there was no meat in the Tropical House until last week, when meat-eating birds arrived.

Thirteen years?
Who did the looking—
another turtle?

Military Sealift Command Probes Munitions Mix-Up

WASHINGTON — The Military Sealift Command Monday was still investigating an incident in which 84 tons of munitions bound for the Middle East ended up at a **Port of New Orleans** shopping mall.

Hey, Bob, these cruise missiles—
do they go to Wicks & Things or Toys R Us?

Lead-Lined Coffins Called Health Risk

Sydney

Australian funeral workers in New South Wales say they are prone to strain injuries because the state insists lead-lined coffins be used for above-ground interments.

"We've had back and shoulder injuries as well as hernias," said Lyle Pepper, head of the New South Wales Funeral and Allied Industries Union.

Gas chambers?
Lead-lined coffins?
Isn't there any safe place?

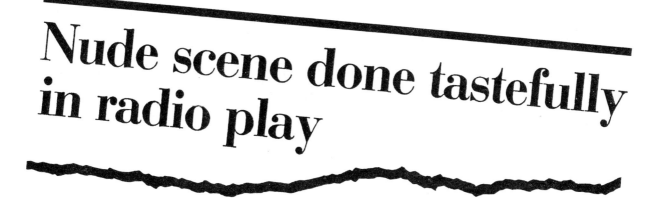

Nude scene done tastefully in radio play

Turn up the volume, Martha, I think they're naked.

Iowa cemeteries are death traps

How many people have to die before we correct this problem?

MGM bounces checks, but says finances OK

Yeah, right, tell it to my landlord.

SMILES to Russell Bellamy and Brent Hertenlehner, both of Port Charlotte, who left their lunch to jump into a canal and save George Bauman, who was floating face-down. Hertenlehner pulled Bauman from the water and Bellamy administered CPR. Such unselfishness on the part of private citizens is commendable.

Imagine—leaving your lunch to save another human being.

Dog was my co-pilot, driver says

SANTA CLARA, Calif. — This is a true story about bad eyes, a barking dog and life in the fast lane.

A visually impaired San Francisco man on Friday tried to convince a judge he wasn't driving solo in the commuter lane, arguing that his dog, Queenie, should count as a second person because she was helping him navigate.

Hey, didn't this guy used to be an umpire and a cabdriver?

Squashed squirrels annoy drivers

ANNAPOLIS (AP) — Squirrels are being squashed in increasing numbers in Maryland and Virginia, annoying and frustrating motorists who try to avoid turning them into road pizza.

Get out of my way. I'm trying to get to the animal rights meeting at the steakhouse.

72 jump into bed
for world record

Has Madonna heard about this?

Nothing destroyed in fire, but damage near $100,000

They were lucky. Imagine what it would have cost
if something *had* been destroyed?

44

A MIND IS A TERRIBLE THING TO WASTE—OR IS IT?

Education, it's often said, is the foundation of a great society. Thus, the importance of school—you know, that place where young people go when things get dull at the mall? To all those dedicated cafeteria workers, crossing guards, and hygiene instructors— these headlines are for you...

"My school's gooder than yours" department:

WHERE
EXCELLANCE
IS
TRADITION

GLENBARD SOUTH HIGH SCHOOL
PARK BOULEVARD & BUTTERFIELD ROAD
GLEN ELLYN, ILLINOIS 60137
PHONE:

Peter J. Abruzzo, Principal

Reeding tutors needed

The Tooele Adult Education instructors need trained tutors to help adults learn to read.

Please apply at Glenbard South High School.

USPS Program Helps to "Stamp Out Literacy"

Gee, I guess reading isn't as important as I thought.

Southwest Baptist University

May 25, 1989

Dear Steven ,

This letter is being sent to you to inform you that your grades for the Spring 1989 semester are being held due to your outstanding account balance. Our records indicate that your account balance as of the date of this letter is $0.00. Your grades are being held in accordance with current University policy and in accordance with the promissory note you signed when registering for the Spring 1989 semester.

It's not the amount of money. It's the principle involved.

49

East Principal Bans Student Mural About Censorship

Wait till he sees the sex ed mural.

Study finds that pupils who attend their classes score markedly better

Hey, you don't think this education thing is working, do you?

Iraq Invades Kuwait; Students May Lose Parking

The ravages of war can affect everyone.

THE CRIMINAL ELEMENT

Criminal vs. cop. It's a confrontation that occurs every day on our city streets: the diabolical criminal, willing to stop at nothing, pitted against our men in blue, schooled in the latest crime-fighting techniques. The following headlines tell the dramatic story...

Cops halt doughnut shop robbery

Hey, why not? They were there anyway.

Fingerprints help cops crack case of the busted piggy bank

David ~~Marshall~~ didn't exactly get caught with his hand in the cookie jar, police say, just with his fingers on the piggy bank.

The Passaic roofer was accused recently of breaking into a Garfield home, ransacking the owner's bedroom, and breaking a porcelain piggy bank cherished by a 3-year-old girl, police say.

He then took the girl's savings, about $5 in pennies, nickels, dimes, and quarters, police say.

"It was a difficult situation; you feel bad for the kid," said Capt. Al

Now, listen to me, Johnson. The mayor's on my back, the newspapers are hounding me. I want answers on this case, and I want them *now*.

Hostage-taker kills self; police shoot each other

The first rule of police work:
never get emotionally involved with a criminal.

Deputy implicated in doughnut theft

Well, Your Honor,
he did have a *glazed* look in his eye.

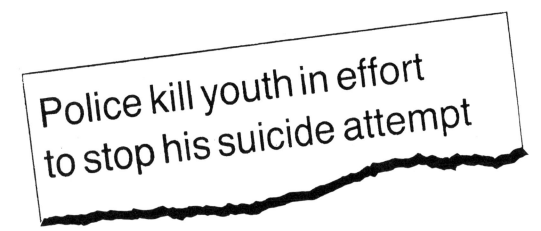

Police kill youth in effort to stop his suicide attempt

They had no choice.
Suicide is against the law.

"Is that a gun or are you happy to see me?" department:

Pants Bulge Provides No Basis for Search

A DIVIDED appellate court has overturned a Manhattan man's drug possession conviction, ruling that an undefined bulge in the man's pants was not suspicious enough to justify a police officer's search and discovery of a bag of cocaine.

"I won't say anything if you don't" department:

Deputy shoots self in butt

URBANA — A Clark County Sheriff's deputy accidently shot himself in his right buttock while attempting to conceal his gun behind his back before searching a Champaign County residence Thursday night.

Naked man trying to buy soda arrested for stealing car

MIDDLESEX—A naked Massachusetts man trying to buy soda at Rick's Sunoco Station was arrested after police discovered the car he was driving was stolen in Brooklyn.

Was it diet soda or regular?

Testicle cargo seized

Ow... I'll talk! I'll talk!

Police kill 2 pit bulls trying to eat live cow

MANNINGTON, W.Va. — Two pit bulls trying to devour a 600-pound cow alive were downed by police bullets as they rushed to attack two officers, collapsing dead just short of their targets.

Basically, they're good little dogs.

"You want fries with that?" department:

Eatery worker arrested after allegedly blowing nose in officer's burger

A 20-year-old fast-food worker has been arrested after he allegedly blew his nose into a hamburger that he served to a Phoenix police officer and then laughed about it.

Man convicted of killing griping diner

BALLSTON SPA, N.Y. — A man who went into a rage after another customer berated a waitress about a cheeseburger served without lettuce and tomatoes was found guilty Wednesday of murdering the complainer.

I bet they won't forget the lettuce and tomato next time.

Theft suspect unable to take off with stolen pigeons in his pants

BALTIMORE — A police officer stopped a man who was walking oddly down the street with bulging pants and found that he had 21 live homing pigeons stuffed in his clothes.

Have the Wright brothers heard of this?

Toy gun scares robber using toy gun

Rochester police on Friday arrested a toy-gun-toting robber who was scared off by the toy gun of one of his victims and then hit on the head by a bat-wielding neighbor.

Good thing they didn't shoot each other. They both could have gotten soaking wet.

Suspect in bank holdups driven by cocaine habit

Police said ███ case is another sad story of crime driven by drug addiction. They described the Winslow Avenue man as a confused and nervous bandit who once left a bank empty-handed because a teller told him he needed to have an account at the branch in order to rob it.

I wonder if this is the same guy who got scared by that toy gun?

Young bunglers try to steal a van filled with policemen

LAKELAND, Fla. — Of all the cars and trucks in the mall's parking lot on one of the year's busiest shopping days, a quartet of would-be car thieves picked on a police surveillance van.

"It was hard to keep from laughing," said Mike Link, one of three officers hiding in the back of the van Saturday when one of the group climbed inside and turned the key.

Boy, and you thought the last guy was stupid.

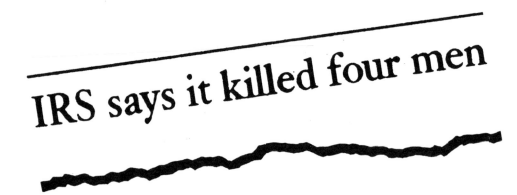

IRS says it killed four men

You ever notice how these stories always come out around tax time?

Woman sits on gun that shoots her

An Issaquah-area woman sat on a gun that shot her on May 15, according to police and fire records.

The 25-year-old woman, who lives between Issaquah and Renton, returned home from a restaurant and was sitting on her bed when she heard a large noise and felt a sharp pain in her rear end, police report. Police discovered she had sat on a .22 caliber pistol that was on the bed.

Do you think she mistook it for a pork chop? (See page 27.)

"We haven't ruled out Mrs. Paul as a suspect" department:

Man allegedly beaten by woman with a frozen fish

Con Sends Death Notes to Judges After Learning to Write in Prison

He's hooked on phonics, Your Honor.

Several Items Reported Stolen From Empty Store

Do you think this is what the typical police report looks like in Moscow?

"A large, shaggy dog was seen lurking in the area" department:

Cat killed by pellet

A Bethlehem cat was killed with a high-powered pellet gun Thursday afternoon, police said.

Bethlehem police investigators are considering the feline's death suspicious.

Bucks man admits attacking house, must go to Florida

Kevin ~~Michael Mogan~~, who pleaded guilty yesterday to attacking his former neighbor's home with a chain saw, will be paroled from prison next week and required to live with his parents in Florida.

Attack a house, go to Florida. It's the law.

Police Beat

Monday morning, a Mt. Desert Street store reported that a white cat had entered the store on three occasions and taken a cat-nip mouse each time. The cat was described as white and wearing a flea color.

A large, shaggy dog was seen lurking in the area.

PENN TOWNSHIP POLICE
FRIDAY

8:30 a.m. A tombstone bearing the name of Sarah J. Moul was found near Hanover Brands. Police are attempting to locate the owner.

PARENTAL GUIDANCE SUGGESTED

With television and radio broadcasting Madonna videos, 2 Live Crew songs, and Depends commercials, those in the newspaper biz can be forgiven if their headlines veer occasionally toward the risqué. But we should be no less vigilant in protecting our children from headlines like the following...

Sorority girls go up and down to benefit Heart Association

Tell me about it.

Penile implants raise hopes

Is this really the best way to phrase this sentence?

Experts test 16,000 condoms

I guess Warren Beatty and Ted Kennedy were busy.

Concord sued over cameras in the potty

SAN FRANCISCO (AP) — The City of Concord has been sued for $30 million because a video camera was placed in the police station men's room.

The suit was filed in U.S. District Court on Tuesday by 29 current and former Concord police officers and civilian employees.

The department installed a hidden video camera above a urinal in 1986, hoping to identify the person who clogged it several times with toilet paper.

Uh, I think we can skip looking at Exhibit A, Your Honor.

Condom instructions require college-level reading ability

Where are the Cliff notes when you really need them?

Man trapped in outhouse overnight 'in ugly mood'

LAWRENCE, Kan. (AP) — After spending a hot summer night at the bottom of an outhouse toilet, a man was pulled free Friday morning unhurt "but in a pretty ugly mood," authorities said.

If we'd had a camera in that potty, this never would have happened.

Investigators crack down on toilet paper offenders

ATLANTIC CITY — The toilet paper cops are making sure the streets of Atlantic City stay clean.

~~Joe Kruger~~ of City Bargains on Atlantic Avenue got more than he bargained for when he tried to sell unmarked rolls of toilet paper and paper towels.

"That's a violation for sure," said Nat Parker, assistant superintendent of the Atlantic City Division of Weights and Measures. "The consumer must know what he's getting."

It's about time they stopped harassing the drug dealers and murderers and went after the real criminals.

IF WE DON'T HAVE IT, WE'LL GET IT!

Recent visitors to the Soviet Union report shocking scarcities—shoe stores with no shoes, butcher shops with no meat. How fortunate that Americans can choose from the bountiful bargains offered here...

I don't even want to know what this is.

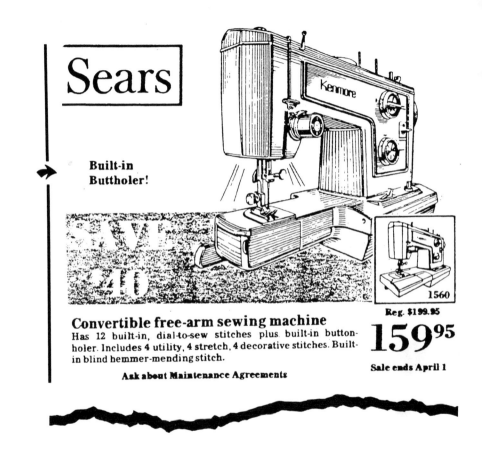

If Timmy is going to school with anything less than an M-1 carbine, he could be unprepared. Don't let your child fall behind.

89

Do you pay extra
for the hot wax?

Sears

OUR GOOD QUALITY
SMOKE ALARM

ITEM NO.: 57361

MODEL NO.: 462 · 57361

OWNERS MANUAL

PLEASE READ CAREFULLY

RESPONDS BEST TO FAST
BURNING, FLAMING FIRES

9 VOLT BATTERY POWERED

Gee, do you have one that responds to smoke?

Let me have two jars of strained carrots and a bottle of Jack Daniels. It's for our three-month-old.

"Revolutionary breakthrough—never needs ironing" department:

Great Buys For Christmas & New Years

New Poly Tuxedos
regularly $175 $129
New All Wood Tuxedos
Values from $250-$595 $199 to $299

For Location Nearest You

HiKEN
FORMAL RENTALS

Nero's GROCERY
COAL & WOOD
SANDWICHES

Here's one way to get more roughage.

Dietrich W. Oellerich Jr., PC
Attorney At Law

10% OFF Free Consultation

Hwy 88, Hephzibah, GA.

Nah, my guy gives 20% off free consultations.

HALLOWEEN Sale!

OVER 1,000,000 ITEMS IN STOCK
10-60% DISCOUNTS ON EVERYTHING

More Styles Than Ever!
Over **200** Accessories, Jewelry and Weapon Choices! • **150** Masks • **100's** of Hats, Wigs and Makeup Disguises • Body Parts and Vermon! • Now More Than **175** Costumes and Kits • Paper Goods • Toys & Give Aways • Lights • Decorations • More!

NINJA TURTLE • JASON • FREDDY • BATHMAN ←

I'll bet the Bathman stuff is *really* discounted.

Why Would Anyone Eat Breakfast Any Place Else?

$299

No Coupon
Necessary

...The Most Fantastic View in Town
...Absolutely Affordable
...All Breakfasts Cooked to Order
...Friendly & Fast Service

OUR DAILY BREAKFAST SPECIAL

2 Eggs, Bacon, Sausage, or Ham, Home Fries & Homemade Biscuits

Oh sure, a good breakfast would run you $500 anywhere else in town.

"Don't go out of your way on my account" department:

"I can't wait to have the rabbi over for dinner" department:

Lose the whole summer?
Hey pal, if that's a
table saw they're using
you could lose
a lot more.

R.W. BY-PRODUCT CO.

Recyclers of Inedible Restaurant Grease

Call for Immediate Service

Boy, I'm getting hungry already.

THE COUPON TABLOID

2 CALZONES
(Stuffed Italian Panties)
Ricotta & Mozzarella + 4 TOPPINGS

$10.39 Plus Tax

DOUBLE DEAL
Pizza

Laguna Lake Center

FREE DELIVERY!
ONE COUPON

with coupon
expires 1/16/91

Yum.

Hey, Mom, remember that Brinks job twenty years ago? Well, this is Susan and she ...

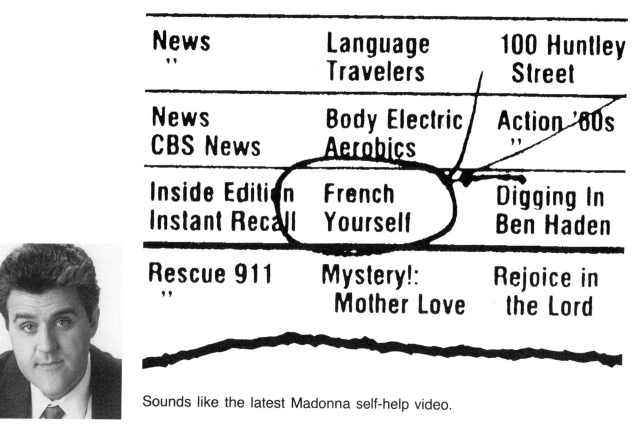

News "	Language Travelers	100 Huntley Street
News CBS News	Body Electric Aerobics	Action '60s "
Inside Edition Instant Recall	French Yourself	Digging In Ben Haden
Rescue 911 "	Mystery!: Mother Love	Rejoice in the Lord

Sounds like the latest Madonna self-help video.

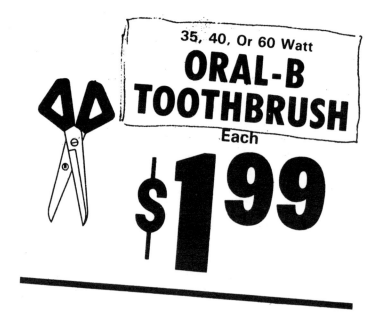

35, 40, Or 60 Watt

ORAL-B
TOOTHBRUSH

Each

$1.99

I think I'll stick to my regular toothbrush, thanks.

CEMETERY PLOTS
2 Butler County
Memorial Park, never
used, $2850. ▮▮▮▮▮▮▮

How much for the used ones?

"Hey, this sausage tastes funny" department:

What a great funeral. I'm stuffed.

Hey, take it easy over those speed bumps, will you?

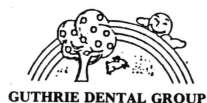
Hello, Doctor.
My Rhode Island red has a serious overbite...

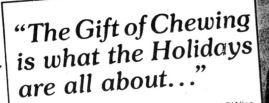

"The Gift of Chewing is what the Holidays are all about…"

James V. D'Alise

Don't let your serious dental problems stop you from enjoying another holiday meal.

Dental Implants can make it possible for you to have attractive, stable teeth and help you to enjoy chewing the foods you desire.

The Center For Dental Implants is having special FREE holiday seminars throughout November and December to show you how easy it is to enjoy the foods you are missing.

ASK ABOUT OUR NEW DENTAL INSURANCE FOR DENTAL IMPLANTS.

The Center for Dental Implants®

Of course it is. It's not about giving or helping someone less fortunate than you. It's about chewing.

CAST YOUR BALLOTS

Many of us envy the politician's life—traveling on junkets, squiring beautiful women around town, receiving kickbacks. But it has its downside, too, as the following headlines show...

White House takes shot at Democrats

A Kuwaiti guards a man identified as an Iraqi army major during questioning in Kuwait City Friday after the suspect was captured at a roadblock. Moments after this picture was taken, the photographer was asked to leave.

Looks like the campaign's starting to heat up.

Captors free Trinidad prime minister
40 still held as Robinson, shot in feet, agrees to step down

Now, be honest. Did you think he would have stepped down if he *hadn't* been shot in the foot?

Rockland incumbents lose; deceased candidate re-elected

Tuesday Elections Will Fill Council, School Board Seats

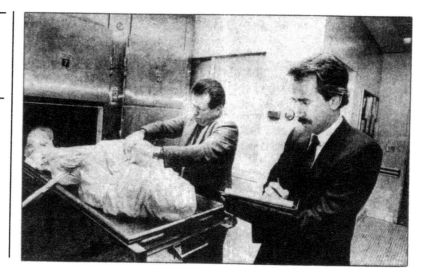

Hey, Doc, check to see whether he's a Democrat or Republican, will you?

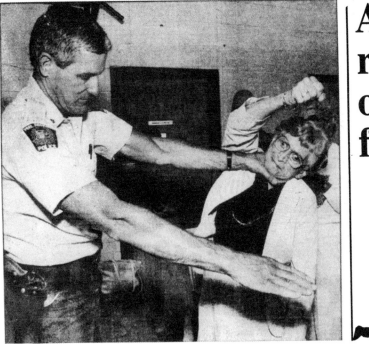

Alderman renews charge of harassment from colleague

Mom, I *told* you not to bother me at the office.

A man holds back tears while another kneels on the ground outside the Imperial Palace in Tokyo early this morning.

AP Laserphoto

Three state congressmen oppose 50% pay increase

You know,
for a minute there
I almost believed them.

White supremacists stumping for top state offices in South

So I guess it's true, all white people do look alike.

IS THERE A DOCTOR IN THE HOUSE?

Any schoolchild can recite the names of the great doctors: Hippocrates, Kildare, Welby. Doctors occupy a special place in society. They command respect. Hence, when their deeds are trumpeted in the local newspaper, we pay close attention.

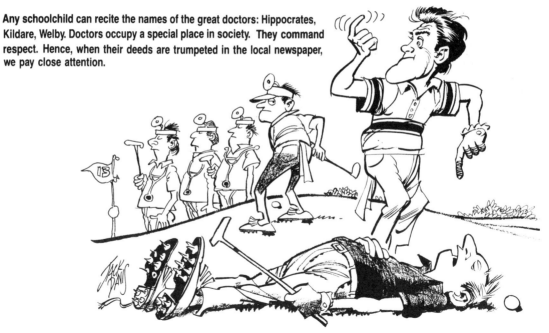

"Could you please pay in advance" department:

Doctors offer suicide guide

From staff and wire reports

BOSTON — Doctors can ethically help terminally ill patients commit suicide by prescribing sleeping pills or other drugs and telling them what dose will end their lives, a panel of prominent doctors concludes.

Foot doctor accused of sucking patient's toe

KEWANEE — A local podiatrist has been charged with battery and disorderly conduct for allegedly sucking the toe of a female patient and making sexually explicit comments and advances to her in his office.

Hey, it works for a snake bite.

In recognition of National Prostate Cancer Week, Stamford urologists **RUDY T. ANDRIANI, M.D.,** and **VINCENT J. TUMINELLO, M.D.,** performed <u>free</u> rectal exams at The Stamford Hospital.

Hello, Betty? Jay. Hey, what are you doing for NPC Week next year? I've got a great idea...

Buzzards cause a buzz

Vultures make unlikely mascots at medical building

If there are vultures
at the entrance, imagine what's
waiting at the exit...

John Everett / Chronicle

Lawrence Frost, studied Custer, ingrown toenails

MONROE, Mich. — Dr. Lawrence A. Frost, a podiatrist and historian who devoted a half-century to studying the life of Gen. George Armstrong Custer, has died. He was 83.

Gee, it's too bad Custer didn't have an ingrown toenail. This guy could have saved himself a lot of research.

"And don't move back here until you get it right" department:

Dentist charged in death sent back to Va. to practice

Hey, Doc, take it easy with that laser...
Nurse, I think he's been drinking again...

Of course the brain was dead. Everyone knows you have to put air holes at the top of the bottle.

Bottled brain found in LSD apartment

A bottle marked "1 whole brain - H - 12-12-83" and containing a human brain in a fluid substance was found by a building custodian at ████ N. Lake Shore Drive.

According to an 18th District Police report, a building custodian found the bottle on a shelf while cleaning out a vacated apartment. A sawed-off shotgun also was found on the premises, the report. **The bottle was taken to Lutheran General Hospital, where the brain was pronounced dead by a physician.** The discovery was made at 11 a.m. on Monday, June 19.

Check with doctors before getting sick

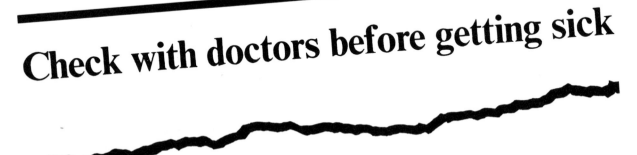

I'm sorry I didn't check with you first, Doc.
I was getting a free rectal exam.

DEATH IS JUST A STATE OF MIND

Among the most newsworthy events in any community is the passing of a loved one. Usually, it's assumed that the deceased will maintain a low profile. But as the following headlines show, the dead often have a lot of living left to do. (Out of respect for the departed, we'll offer no comment.)

Dead Man
Gets Job Back

SYDNEY, Australia (AP) — A man who died while going to a hearing to fight his job dismissal has been reinstated to the job.

Dead man still goes duck hunting with pal

FARMINGTON, Ill. (AP) — Dean Goddin died in the mid-1980s, but that hasn't made him miss a single day of duck hunting with his buddy, Everett Staffeldt.

In keeping with his last request, Goddin's ashes were placed inside a pair of 2-foot mallard duck decoys that Staffeldt, a retired scientist, had originally carved for his own remains.

Dead man found in cemetery

Tax collectors decide to leave dead man alone

OMAHA, Neb. — The IRS says it has decided not to exhume the body of an Iranian businessman who allegedly owed the government $157,000 when he died.

Dead man remains dead

CITY OF INDUSTRY, Calif.
A man apparently died while visiting a spiritual medium, who then spent a week trying to revive him, authorities said.

YOU CAN FIND IT IN THE CLASSIFIEDS

Where can you find a great buy on cellophane underwear, a job sucking the seeds out of watermelons, a lover who is ambidextrous? Why, the classifieds, of course. Take a look at these tempting offers...

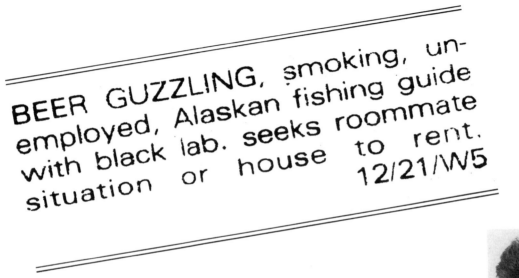

BEER GUZZLING, smoking, un-employed, Alaskan fishing guide with black lab. seeks roommate situation or house to rent. 12/21/W5

Please, don't everyone call at once.

Musician Wanted: Avondale Lutheran Church is looking for a pianist for Sunday morning worship services at 9 and 10:30 a.m. Must know how to play the piano in Spanish. Contact (███) ███████.

Well, my specialty's Canadian, but I can get by in Spanish.

MODERATELY intelligent, occasionally nice professional male in early 40s seeks educated unencumbered woman with sense of humor & a backpack. If ex-husband in prison, please include release date.

Dear Nice Professional Man:
My husband is a beer-guzzling
Alaskan fishing guide.
He'll be out of prison Thursday.
Hope to hear from you.
P.S. He'll have the backpack with him.

HELP WANTED: Door to door, selling oranges, apples, grape-fruit. No experience needed, will train, paid daily. <u>Prefer female or male.</u> Call ▓▓▓▓▓ Room 21. After 8 p.m., ask for Mr. King.   31-7

Hey, what if you *have* experience, but aren't male or female? Can you still get the job?

$35,000 *plus* women! Can I see what they look like first?

MIRIAM, as a token of my undying love, I'm knocking a $120 off what you still owe me. Your big Bear **WES.**

Who says men aren't romantic?

FOUND false teeth, lower plate, good condition. Contact the Flemingsburg Sewer Plant, ▓▓-▓▓. sept19c

Mildred, I left my false teeth on the toilet.
Have you seen them?

LOST DIAPER BAG: With very sentimental items. In Taco Bell Parking Lot, Jackson. 7/8/90. Reward ███-████.

Boy, they must be *very* sentimental items.

LOST in Gotham Area. One pair of used men's under- wear. Call D.J.'s Kwik Stop if found.

Lost in Gotham? Holy briefs, Batman!

FOR BETTER OR FOR WORSE

It's been said that a couple never looks more attractive than the day they're married. Perhaps it's the joy of seeing a dream fulfilled, perhaps it's the thought of all that money in the envelope from Uncle Ned. The following headlines celebrate that most sacred of institutions: marriage.

Hogg and Hamm to Exchange Vows

Mr. and Mrs. Hugh W. Hogg of Leedey, are proud to announce the engagement and approaching marriage of their daughter, Susan Kay, to Russel G. Hamm of Weatherford. Russel is the son of Mr. and Mrs. Gene Hamm also of Weatherford.

I bet their kid's going to be a little porker.

Wong-Wright wedding plans announced

CEDAR FALLS — Announcement is being made of the engagement and approaching marriage of Siew-San Wong and Steven Wright.

Well, the nice thing is, you only need one set of monogrammed bath towels.

Associated Press

Happily married for 74 years

Sylvia Simmons, 93, and husband Ernie, 96, celebrated their 74th wedding anniversary at a Colorado Springs nursing home over the weekend. The couple were married during a blizzard in Garden City, Kan., in 1916.

You know,
it's written
all over
their faces.

Wife regrets staying with man she killed

She regrets it? How about him?

WEDDINGS

Last-Fling

Katherine Andrea Last and Joseph George Fling were married in the chapel of the Church of the Good Samaritan, Paoli, Jan. 20. Officiating were the Rev. Lucinda Laird, the bride's cousin, and the Rev. Russell Sherman.

This marriage should last—unless, of course, he decides to have a fling.

Man Discovers He Left Wife At Local Station

A Texas man arrived at the home of relatives in Oklahoma City at about noon Friday to be informed he had driven away from Perry without missing his wife, leaving her at a local service station.

Woman scolded for killing husband

MOUNT CLEMENS, Mich. (AP) — A Macomb County woman received five years of probation and a scolding for stabbing her husband to death as he tried to strangle her.

"If you had an ounce of common sense in your head at all, you should have known what you were getting into," Macomb Circuit Judge Deneweth told Gay Hill, 46, at her sentencing Friday. She was also sentenced to receive mental-health counseling and told to get a job.

I tell you, if more murderers got a good scolding, there'd be less crime in this country.

COMMUNITY AFFAIRS

Experts tell us that community spirit is built through shared activity. Potluck suppers, "Meet the Candidates" nights, gatherings where men wear funny hats and get liquored up; it's events such as these that bring us together and make for a lifestyle that can't be beat. The following headlines show just how many different types of activities Americans get involved in...

OPEN HOUSE

The City of Hays has scheduled an Open House on Friday, December 21, 1990, at the Sewage Treatment Plant located on East Hwy. 40 Bypass, from 9:00 a.m. to 5:00 p.m.

Refreshments Will Be Served

Hey, anybody find a set of false teeth?

DAUGHTER'S MEETING – All women who have <u>served the country during the Revolution or was the mother of a patriot</u> are invited to a coffee at 9:30 a.m. on Monday, Oct. 29 at Our Place Restaurant, First Interstate Bank Building, Carefree. The purpose of the meeting is to establish a Desert Foothills chapter of the Daughters of the American Revolution.

I hear Betsy Ross's mother will be there. It could be fun.

Civil War returns at encampment

Re-enactments of both military and civilian activities will be held. Groups of trained infantry and artillery, dressed in period costumes, will conduct military demonstrations. Other period activities will include a political debate and a church service.

There will also be presentations by the U.S. Corps of Engineers, the U.S. Sanitary Commission, and the camp chaplain Lancaster's own Maj. Gen. John F. Reynolds, the first officer killed in Gettysburg, will be on hand.

Hey, maybe we can fix him up with one of those Revolutionary War gals.

Fort Collins fails in quest for bigger dot on map

FORT COLLINS, Colo. (AP) — Fort Collins' "big dot committee" failed to win the city a bigger dot in Rand McNally's "Road Atlas 1989," but members who believe the city's pride is at stake have vowed to keep fighting.

Oh well, there's always next year.

4-H cow pie bingo to be held at Kittson County Fair

Believe me, you don't want to know.

CHRISTMAS DAY POTLUCK

December 25   11-4:00

Bring a dish! **KAUL FUNERAL HOME** will provide the meats. Sign up NOW, if you are interested. Registration at front counter.

And you thought cow-pie bingo was hard to stomach.

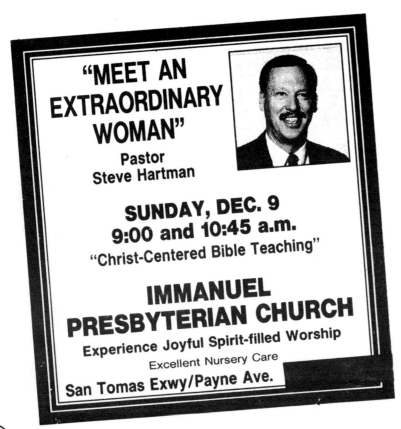

"MEET AN EXTRAORDINARY WOMAN"

Pastor
Steve Hartman

SUNDAY, DEC. 9
9:00 and 10:45 a.m.
"Christ-Centered Bible Teaching"

IMMANUEL
PRESBYTERIAN CHURCH
Experience Joyful Spirit-filled Worship
Excellent Nursery Care
San Tomas Exwy/Payne Ave.

Gee, just the fact that she has a mustache makes her an extraordinary woman.

NEW DOG TRAINING CLASS

10 Weeks - $25.00

SIGN-UP NIGHT
MON., JUNE 19

**6:00 p.m.
At the
WAUSHARA COUNTY
FAIRGROUNDS**
(By the Livestock Building)
**Bring Leashes, Collars
& Shot Records
(No Dogs)**
*(Sponsored by Waushara
County Kennel Club)*

What happens next Monday?
Just dogs, no owners?

Missouri woman big winner at hog show

Uh, lady, I wouldn't brag about this too much.

PHOTO OPPORTUNITIES

For this last chapter, I've saved my favorite photos—either those that appeared next to an unrelated headline, or those that found their way into print precisely because they were so strange. Follow me, won't you, to The Headline Gallery...

Troops take positions

We're looking for
a few good men.

Africanized Bee threat distorted, keeper says

They travel in massive swarms devouring everything in their path with deadly stings.

That's a common notion many people have about the Africanized Honey Bee - also known as the "killer bee" - which is expected to penetrate United States borders from Mexico by 1992.

Just wait till they grow to full size.

BRETT ALLISON FLEET/STAFF PHOTOGRAPHER

Roger Stewart, 25, of Corpus Christi holds up his cousin Andrew Canales, 3, to get a good look at the bee who represents the Reginal Transportation Au thority during the annual 16 de Septiembre Parade Sunday evening. The parade commemorated the anniversary of Mexico's independence from Spain.

Big Roll? Looks like they're going to need a couple *Extra*-Big Rolls.

Developer fights for Hamilton traffic study

Okay, keep coming...keep coming...HOLD IT!

LEAVING AFGHANISTAN

PHILIPPE WOJAZER/Reuters

An Afghan refugee digs a hole in front of his tent near Peshawar, Pakistan, on Thursday as the flood of refugees continued. Rebel rockets killed seven people in Kabul despite the withdrawal of Soviet troops from Afghanistan.

All right . . . that's it.
I'm out of here.

Wildlife Officials Working on Plan to Help Pheasants

Gene Hornbeck/World-Herald

Pheasants could prove more plentiful after a Game and Parks plan is implemented ... A final draft will be presented to the seven-member governing board of the commission for its approval in late summer or early fall.

Gee, I wonder if these are the same officials who came up with that plan to count the dead fish by poisoning the rivers. (See page 17.)

WINTRY RIDE — An Amish buggy makes its way along Hawley Road just south of Scottville, last week, amid frigid temperatures and blowing snow.

BUREAU PHOTO • BRIAN MASCK

MSU student launches video delivery service

If you don't get it in thirty days or less, it's free.

Bombing range opening to public

(AF Laserphotos)

GILA BEND, Ariz. (AP) — The Air Force, Marines and a few federal agencies are putting out the welcome mat on a gunnery range twice the size of Delaware and legendary for its contradictions.

Inviting greater public use of the Barry M. Goldwater Air Force Range might appear the greatest contradiction of all: The 2.7 million-acre preserve, described as the free world's largest target range, contains seven areas where fighters strafe and bomb simulated trains, convoys and missile bases. It has three more for practicing aerial dogfights.

An information packet which includes an agreement absolving the military of any harm to the visitor refers to unexploded ordnance dating back to the 1940s and warns that "munitions items are designed to maim and kill."

Put off by the crowds at Disney World? Bored by the serenity of Yosemite? Why not put a little duck-and-cover into your backpacking?

Homeless live out Cinderella fantasy

Associated Press

President and Barbara Bush danced during an inaugural ball Friday at the Washington Convention Center.

Okay, you pretend you're the president and I'll pretend I'm the first lady...

Stay with me, Raisa, and I'll get you nylons, chocolates, and toilet paper.

President Bush leads Raisa Gorbachev by the arm as Barbara Bush and Soviet President Gorbachev assemble for a group photograph Saturday at Camp David. The group was scheduled to spend the day at the mountain retreat.

AP

Americans grab summit opportunities

"Airline passengers sick of being treated like cattle" department:

Nosed off plane, 'smelly' pair sues airline

Associated Press

WATERTOWN, N.Y. — A couple kicked off a USAir flight after an attendant complained they smelled bad are asking the airline for an apology and the price of two of its most expensive tickets.

"Personally, I don't think we smelled any different than anybody else on the plane," Randi ~~Freeman~~ said Tuesday. She

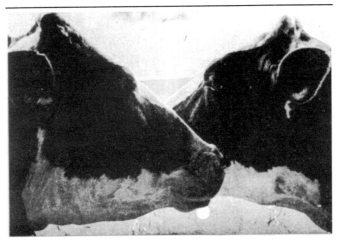

Davidsville's Main Street is a hub of activity in the village.

Todd Berkey/The Tribune-Democrat

Oh, sure, it's busy now, but you should see it on a Sunday morning.

Ah, a little paint here,
a little plaster there...

Let's face it,
when your family
starts growing,
you need a bigger
house.

Courier-Post photo by Evangelos Dousmanis

"Look, we're trying to find a better name" department:

I don't know how you play it, I don't care how you play it, and I don't want to see anyone else play it.

Give the people what they want.

Gee, that would look nice, wouldn't it—
a big wheel of cheese hanging over your fireplace?

"Some things are just too good to pass up" department:

Ya—uberburger!

It's up to each of us
to keep our dump neat.

And people wonder why the banking industry in this country is falling apart.

Welcome to the Twilight Zone....